Lessons from the Trials of Life

Carl Rice

Kellogg Press   Topeka, KS

Lessons from the Trials of Life
Copyright © 2021 Carl Rice

Published by Kellogg Press
Topeka, KS
www.kelloggpress.com

Curtis Becker, Editor/Design
curtis@curtisbeckerbooks.com

All rights reserved. No part of this publication may be reproduced, distributed, or transmitted in any form or by any means, without prior written permission of the copyright holder.

Printed in the United States of America

Adobe Georgia Font

Photography by Carl Rice, Curtis Becker, Chris Kelley, Michelle Pringle, James Obernesser (Unsplash), and Dave Hoefer (Unsplash). Used by permission. Additional photographs from Shutterstock or Rice family archives. Shutterstock User ID: 301765167

Cover by Curtis Becker and Chris Kelley

ISBN: 978-0-578-92245-4

Lessons from the Trials of Life

Prelude

I coached two Navajo youth early in my career. They were reservation youngsters who had rough lives. Their grandparents were raising them. The grandparents were stable if not limiting factors in lives that were caught between two conflicting realities. These two boys spent formative time on the Window Rock Reservation and their scholastic time with surrogate parents in our district. They played football on my teams, and I became familiar with not only the boys but with their grandparents. The matriarch was not overly pleased with their participation. I became friendly with and appreciative of her while advocating for her Grandsons.

She often called me Shush. I didn't take the time to get clarification for the title but felt certain derisiveness when I first heard it. Only after a considerable time did I notice that the raspiness had softened when it was uttered. I finally asked Leo, the older of the boys, what it meant. He laughed and said it had a couple of meanings: 1. A big hairy man. 2. A scary big Bear. I asked which one she meant, and he smiled and said that I got to choose. Later, I learned that the big hairy man was not a compliment but the bear might be.

I actually liked the definitions and I grew to adore her. I accepted and used the name for my writing.

1

My father loved in a confusing unsettling way. We spent our early days in many houses while Dad worked for many different people. We were poor but generally happy and we thought we were the center of everything. Dad adored his boys. He dreamed of the day they would be great ball players or great musicians or just great Dads. He was a great Dad; he gave all that he had even though he had little.

Dad worked and Mom took care of the house and the boys. There was a cloistered sadness in her that was never obvious unless you watched her closely. She seemed at times remote and grudging. She lived as if she carried a very heavy burden and often seemed not to want to be where we were. She was a good mother; she gave what she had even though she had little.

We moved from remote place to remote place. My father worked for land owners until he was either bored or until disagreement determined that a separation was necessary. He was a ranch hand for numerous owners, a logger, a mechanic, a farmer, a manager of a gas station, and a deputy sheriff.

Each change necessitated physical moves. Looking back, I wonder if he was chasing a dream or escaping. I cannot speak for my brothers, but I developed certain distrust for the physical environment. I knew I was loved by my parents, but I was distressed because I would just get comfortable with friends, teachers, and communities when a major change would be forced upon me. At times it seemed that my parents were so busy loading and unloading our old GMC truck, that they had very little time for the comparative and trivial problems of the masculine hatch for which they were responsible.

We grew up in two worlds, the formulated world of our home and the world that surrounded us. The latter was ever-changing and mostly threatening. I could never get comfortable within it but I did learn to manage its inconsistencies by observing and mimicking the most successful of my cohorts. I sometimes felt alone at home, I mostly felt alone when I was "out there."

Pleasant Surprise

Over by the garden
I planted a new tree.
I waited and waited for it to grow,
but it didn't as far as I could see.

I walked by the twig often
on my way to where I went.
I always thought I had wasted
the money I had spent.

I can't tell you why I didn't pull it up,
why I didn't burn it with the weeds and grass that
    I had cut.
It stood alone through cold and snow
and was there to greet me when the winter broke.

I had lots of things to do, mend the fence,
and paint the barn, and get the fields ready for
    the warmth.
The stark stick stood,
no time had I for this worthless plant.

I didn't take the time to pull it up
and put it in the trash.

Carl Rice

  I did my work and went away
for some time of fun and happy days.

I turned back home when I was done
but I had burned a lot of suns.
My fun had kept me fast away
and home had changed when ere I came.
The house was peeled, the barn was gone,
and the land around was mostly ruined.

I turned to go and caught my breath
for the wonder I did see!
The garden spot grew high with weeds,
beneath the limbs of a mighty tree.

-Shush

It is amazing how often the things of little consequence turn out to be the greatest things in life.

Lessons from the Trials of Life

*Mildred Pearl Arbogaste
20 years old*

*Cecil Rice
Cowboy, Baseball Player, Philosopher, and dad*

Old Rock School, Piceance Creek, CO
Started school in this building. First and second grade teacher was Beverly Gentry.

2

My brothers were a curious lot. They were a menagerie of personality strengths and weaknesses. In each was an indelible strength and resolve, qualities born of need and genetic stubbornness. Each possessed a fallibility that was hard to perceive and define. My brothers, to a person, were good people who fought the good fight. They grew to be contributors if not needy contributors while living like they had a hole in them. yet, they lived exemplary lives. They were teachers, successful business men, and good fathers. I love them all and am proud of them; they give what they have even when they have little.

The truth is that your life has to have some control. The conservative nature of our species has allowed us to flourish. The folks who get to majority have either been lucky or have observed reasonable constraint and eventual restraint.

We had obvious constraints that we thought were debilitating. We wore patched clothing. We took baths in a tub in front of the stove, thus, on limited occasions. We couldn't afford school lunches so we carried our own lunches to school. The lunches were often butter sandwiches and were a source of perceived embarrassment. We usually lived far from town and thus had difficulty in joining our peers for social endeavors. We were all boys, no girls, and as such were bereft of opportunity to even partially understand more than half of our community. Expected to work soon after learning to walk, we found we had chores. These were jobs that were delegated to youngsters based on their developing abilities and on whether they were disgusting enough that the parents chose not to deal with them. Feeding the hogs--, who always had to be located in a pen far enough away from the house as to limit the smell--, and cleaning the chicken house were examples of the most onerous tasks assigned. The mundane necessary tasks, gathering eggs, milking, and feeding were easy but demanded ultimate consideration from any schedule. I remember, when we were pre-high school, how problematic these tasks were because they demanded consistent attention at all costs. I remember thinking how much they kept me from having fun like other kids.

I knew my brothers felt the same way as they traveled through their personal journeys. Each of their perspectives regarding these variables was shaped not only by their unique gifts but by watching the travails of their older brothers. Each of them flourished or receded based on resolutions that they alone developed. Our constraints though disliked never truly defamed us, they in fact simply slowed us down enough to allow true evaluation.

Constraints lead to restraints that can be good or bad. Restraints slow you down;, you ponder the value and validity; they keep you from jumping to conclusions and making big mistakes. They can also keep you from taking needed chances and being creative. Wisdom comes from understanding that your resolutions flow from a predetermined cast. The cast that was created, as you grew and resolved your experiences, it tended to determine direction and spontaneity for the rest of your life. Each time you are presented with a challenge or an out of the ordinary emotion you respond like it is a butter sandwich. It is seldom taken for the simple and enduring reason that it was given to you but is evaluated based on its enduring emotional result. I resolved that it was safer and natural to be shrouded in the background yet, I was given talents that occasionally made me stand out.

Tommy in the Window

His uniform all neat and clean,
his hair is combed just right.
This picture of a wishful lad is
almost as big as life.

We hung it on the glass up front,
a sight for all to see,
a pretentious boy whose likeness spoke
of a life he could but dream.

We laughed and teased this innocent,
embarrassment for gall.
To dare to state his fragile dreams
in a picture on the wall.

Then as if to rub it in
we called him forth to see,
the folly of his boisterous deed,
the object of his dream.

The innocent with smile of trust
when beckoned forth did come.
He took our taunts with thoughtful gaze
and acted nonchalant.

Lessons from the Trials of Life

But as he turned to flee the scene,
I saw his hurt eyes drop.
In certain shame he walked away,
a lesson ill but taught.

What have I done, I thought aloud?
A stupid fool am I!!
A young boys dream I may have cursed,
an idle deed awry.

The courage that it takes to dream,
to be the epic man,
is often crushed to death
by the simple phrase you can't.

The picture in the window is his work of art.

Tommy in the window is Sir Thomas in his heart!

Shush

Where dreams are built! Practice.

3

My earliest recollection of true and vibrant life was when I was allowed to go to work with my father. I escaped the confines of the house and its matriarchal dominance and entered into masculine reality. My earliest memories of those adventures were of accompanying my father as he fed cattle, of spending nights with him in a camp as he irrigated for bosses that he worked for, or of taking the logging horses to Green Mountain to skid logs.

I remember being buried in the hay on the hay

rack to keep me warm as he loaded the rest of the rack with sweet smelling hay. I remember getting to drive the team down the road when we were coming home and of thinking what a hand I was. It didn't dawn on me that the team would have gone home, on its own.

I remember playing in the ditch and catching fish while Dad was irrigating at Kiowa, Colorado. I remember playing checkers with him in between sets. We used buttons for pieces, and sometimes I won. I was amazed at my ability because I had seldom seen him lose to others he played against. It didn't dawn on me that he was letting me win.

I remember accompanying him when he was logging in the mountains above Lagarita. My job was to keep the jays away from the lunch, this was accomplished with ill placed thrown rocks that never hit a single bird. When the day was done, I had the task of riding Marge, our old bay logging mare, back to our cabin. I would ride behind the hames and hold the halter while directing the huge old mare on the path leading down the mountain. It didn't dawn on me that old Marge was actually more knowledgeable about the path homeward than I, and that she would have gone home on her own.

I went with Dad to farm, to brand, to build fence, to fix wind mills, to build barns, to herd cattle, and a multitude of other jobs that seemed simple when he was working them. I pitched in with small parts of those tasks, and I thought that my role was irreplaceable. The truth never occurred, or was expressed, that the job would have been accomplished without my contribution.

Later, I learned that these tasks not only required talent and knowledge but extreme physical prowess. My father's work was ridiculously taxing and he was engaged so for endless hours. He came home dead tired and re-engaged the next day, for what had to seem like an endless sentence. The amazing thing, that has never escaped my memories, is the number of times he arrived at the end of one of those trying days and grabbed a bat and a baseball. He would finish the day hitting fly balls to any of his boys that cared to be involved. His love for us was an active love. He didn't say it with words but his actions screamed his intentions.

He loved us all and gave what he had even when he had little.

Anthem

This night I sit alone and ponder
our collected plight.
Why does living seem so different
than in my younger life?

All things are rushed till time is spent,
and then rest is rushed anew.
Days and nights become a blur
and seasons pass too soon.

Then near the end
one day arrives when
weathered and forlorn old souls
review their trifling lives.

They wonder why, when nearly spent,
they've nothing here to give.
They look back on hollow lives
and yearn for what they've missed.

They fashion up beguiling lies
to tell of efforts strong,
to try to leave behind their gift
to stay forever young.

Their stories speak of riches gained,
and fame and sated lusts.
Yet soon the truth reveals itself
these chants will turn to dust.

A simple lesson slipped away
beneath the march of time,
a picture on the attic floor
beneath the artifacts of life.

A Father sitting on a porch
in the colored evening light,
upon his knee there sits a lad
in loving arms held tight.

Carl Rice

The boy beholds all truth and good,
he questions not the talk.
He listens with reverence
of a subject to his God.

He hears the truth of life lived long
that's lovingly portrayed
to tender ears that question not,
the mind to be engraved.

Yes the truth is stretched a bit,
there's a twinkle in the eye,
when adventures past and feats of might
are recounted on this night.

This communion is made special;
it's the passing of the torch.
It's the timeless truth of struggles bold;
it's our journey on this earth.

The chain of life is built the same,
the father to the son.
Each link profound is forged
within the bounds of human love.

The legends of the struggle dare
define all wrong and right,
they give the young the fuel
to carry on the fight.

Lessons from the Trials of Life

Woe is to him who breaks this chain,
what reason he may claim.
Be it haste to make a dollar
or avarice the shame.

A simple way to sit in shade
is to plant and grow the tree.
You plant it where it's safe
and provide its basic needs.

The lad upon his Father's lap
extends his family tree.
The time that's spent will bear good fruit,
the goodness we will reap.

Most answers to the trials of life,
are at our fingertips,
in the attic on the floor,
beneath the dust and chips.

 The picture of a loving man
beneath the setting sun,
the answer in a question. . .

Where have our Father's gone?

Shush

Carl Rice

Hayrides and work

Baseball afterward

4

My mother was a mystery to me. She was what we now call a stay at home mother, and was responsible for a household full of boys. She was seldom afforded the luxury of luxury. We were poor, and she was surrounded by children that she had created biannually. A boy every two years was brought into her world, a world where there was never enough creature comforts to embrace and never enough time to appreciate blessings. She was adept at problem solving and social creativity but seldom seemed gentle or happy.

Mom tried to manage with fear. Brooms, fly

swatters, kitchen tools, and objects that could be hurled, were implements that had dual purposes. The first was the intended, and the second was an agent for equalizing any disparity in size or number. Mom could have written a book on the way to use items for punishing iniquitous boys. She was never lethal but always effective.

We were careful when dealing with her directly because her view of right was what she decided. I remember the difficulty that she had when her boys started getting so big that she was not able to thrash them as soundly as she felt they might deserve. Some of my less experienced siblings thought that power had shifted and that they might not have to be as attentive to her will as they had previously been forced. All underestimated her ability to adapt.

She found subtle ways to coerce and control emotions and occasionally had brilliant responses to overt acts. An example was when my brother came home after curfew when he was first ordained as both a driver and an owner of his very own car. He was confronted by mom, who had been awake, worrying or stewing, for a few hours. He had no good excuse for his sin and was asked for his keys and told he was grounded. His reply was that the keys were his and he would not give them to her. He smugly turned and went to bed.

He awakened the following morning, attended to his morning rituals and went to his car to go to school. His car was jacked up, had all four wheels removed, and was resting on blocks. The wheels were nowhere to be seen. He later discovered they were resting in the garage and the door to such garage was locked. The key was not available to him because it belonged to his mother. A month later she graciously afforded him the key and he was able to re-wheel his very own car.

Mom said she loved all her boys. She never said it a lot to them, but she readily attested the fact to others. She was fiercely protective of all her brood and was a prime example of an agent that might deal with you stringently within the confines of home, but God save anybody from without that might lay prey on any of her family.

I remember her stopping a trucker during harvest that was speeding on the road in front of our house. She told him that she had little kids, and that he was going too fast too close to her home. He correctly responded that he was going the speed limit. The conversation escalated to yelling and the truck driver eventually left in fit of anger. Mom calmly went to the shop and retrieved a shovel and a bar. She spent a good deal of the evening using the shovel and the bar and an extension of the water hose to dig a prolific ditch across the road. The following morning the same truck driver nearly wrecked when he crossed the ditch on his way to the wheat field. Point made; he didn't stop, but slowed to a crawl while hauling his final loads.

She corrected teachers, coaches, and neighbors who might defame her boys. Those efforts were generally followed by some form of private correction at home. We didn't get away with much if she knew about our mistakes.

Mom's life was a history of difficulty. Her mother died suddenly when she was five years old. She and her older sister were raised by an adoring and responsible father. She worked, like a man, with her father on a small farm in southern Colorado. I think sometimes she was treated like a son as much as a daughter. I know she could fix any old car or piece of machinery. She also had a masculine gruffness that accentuated her personality. She was confrontational, and perceptive, and sometimes unpredictable. She never had much but she gave all she had even when she had little.

Pearl

She's here again,
awake at dawn,
to fashion a new day.

The tasks are here,
they demand her time,
and she toils to find a way.

She has no time,
to take some time,
to breathe and try to care.

Her life's not hers
to give away
her passion not to share.

Where is her heart
the question fair,
unanswered still we know.

Hidden deep
within her heart,
where only she can go.

The place to be
when times are kept to her
and her alone.

The sadness sweeps
across her brow
like the cold before the storm.

The place where
fear and pain and guilt
abide within the walls.

Carl Rice

The offending cries
and hurt filled eyes
that call please take me home.

She lives with this
while serving them
that cannot understand.

The pain and strife
that fill her life
behind her daily stand.

She struggles through
unending times
her service is required.

The head of house,
the gentle mom,
the chaste and loving wife.

Her life's not hers
to give away
her passion not to share.

The thin and present veil
 that always
keeps her here.

Her life is long,
her trial cold,
her resolution made.

She has few gifts
to give away
in her final days.

Yet she toils to build
some gifts for those
whom she has made.

A final gesture
small but grand
before she goes away.

Give her grace
and take some time
to try to understand.

Her time and life
long gone away
her pain still close at hand.

She loved and gave
what she had each day
she kept us here.

Carl Rice

I prayed the day
she cried and left
that peace would follow her.

Shush

Mother and crew

Lessons from the Trials of Life

5

As humans, I think we are all on a trek to discover our place in this world. We have volumes of defense mechanisms to shroud our insecurities. We seldom expose what we really feel and we either hide or we crow to diffuse discovery. I have never totally understood how we are ordained to act under daily pressures but I think realistically we mimic our environment. We are didactic. We gather information from our models and apply the same tactics. If those tactics work we simply refine the behaviors and carry on.

    My brothers and I lived in the fog between our

extended families. One family didn't want us, and the other we chose to separate from. We were a unit to ourselves most of the time, and even though we heard stories of the branches, we were seldom given the opportunity to examine our heritage. I grew to wonder why and question. I was never brave enough to ask outright, but I felt like something was missing.

My younger brothers grew to be fine boys. I appreciated the innocence that was obvious in each of them and thought about the rhythm that families created; I was proud of mine and simultaneously suspicious. I wondered why we spent so little time with my dad's family and why we seemed so different from mother's. I wondered why there was a tension when we were with either of them.

I adored both of my grandfathers and didn't know either of my grandmothers. My aunts and uncles were a mystery to me, and to be honest, were never integral or interested in mine or my brother's lives. Normal always was away from them, and to be honest, was a lot less complicated than when we were forced to attend a rare occasion. I always enjoyed the fried chicken and never cared for the pretended acceptance that we were afforded.

In time, I rebelled. I tried to fight; my anger drove my life. I couldn't control the urge I had to deny my home. I wanted to find a place to escape the intrigue, a place where quiet could rule, and maybe one could get some positive attention. My temper reigned when I was challenged, and I forgot the strength and resolve that my parents modeled daily. My father counseled me on many occasions about control and service. I remember when he discussed with me my urge to use my physical strength on others. He told me that "It takes the greatest strength to be gentle. " Initially that lesson was lost on me but life has a way of revealing truths.

You Can't Beat This Guy

You're a long way from right
and a left turn from wrong.
Yet you think you've figured it out.

You can't find your way
and you don't know yourself,
and you reek of philosophical doubt.

What are your thoughts
and why should I care,
since you can't give a damn for the truth?

Who is your shield
and why should I trust,
when your reason is short in the tooth?

Carl Rice

So here we both sit
with our hair ruffled up,
and our ire up in each other's face.

We have lost all hope
of forgiving the grief
that epitomizes a break of good faith.

I can't see your point
because you won't take a chance
to see if your truth is true.

You just forge ahead
with no thought of your course,
we could talk 'til our faces turn blue.

Here we stand
with our hearts beating fast
and our fists clenched with righteous rage,

We're about to find out
if your will or mine
will decide the words of the page.

I'm not sure if you want
to take this step
to test your will and my nerve,

Lessons from the Trials of Life

and I'm really not sure
if I care enough
to give you the hell you deserve.

All muscled up
you step in my space
with a hideous scowl on your face.

We swing and we hack,
we grunt and we groan,
we break stuff all over the place.

When were all done
and our muscles are spent
and our brain catches up with our fear.

We stand there all done
with our arms hanging down
and no resolution that's clear.

I can't go again
yet I know you are wrong,
so I choose to postpone the blaspheme.

We go on our way
without the resolve
that a good war should most often bring.

Carl Rice

I open the door
and walk to the street.
I think as I amble along.

Who won?
Who knows and who knows what's right?
The reason is definitely gone.

Except for the knot
that protrudes from my head
no remnants remain of a fight.

Tomorrow I'll act
like nothing has changed
and everything's going alright.

I hate this lull,
this lack of resolve,
in a lie I seem to be caught.

A passionate spill,
a waste of my time,
a lesson that cannot be taught,

My life will go on
and I'll not take the time
to remember or care for this cause.

Lessons from the Trials of Life

It's all in your hands
what happens to you,
so take some time for your thoughts.

You do as you wish,
you can laugh and move on,
or bitch till your face turns blue.

Reacting to "dumb"
is a waste of my time
so here's a hearty "SCREW YOU!"

Shush

It has been my experience that when the fighting starts you have lost the chance for a solution.

6

I thought I had it figured out; my family might be wrong. I spent some time alone and made my own rules and often made mistakes that made recovery difficult. I needed help but I didn't choose to rely on my family.

I was lucky enough to be embraced by some folks that seemed to have life figured out. I was adopted by significance and relativity. I saw the other side, the "correct side." I realized that not everyone had holes and few lived in the fog. I thought that where I went was where it was. The answers became the opposite of the experiences that I had endured. The light entered my life and I was surrounded by what I thought folks should be. I moved in with a well-to-do family and was embraced by them. They noticed me; they attended to my needs; and they seemed to believe in me. Whole people did exist and I was part of them. They gave some of what they had, and they had a lot to give.

I intuitively compared my new existence to my birth family. I reveled in my good luck at being included in their midst. The initial comparison was illegitimate. They had a big house and new car. They could actually buy groceries when they were needed and didn't have to wait until payday. They could afford clothes that were in style and not likely to cause embarrassment. They had little physical stress, they were definitely not limited by their environment. How blessed they seemed. They were obviously above the simple existence that I had endured.

Time passed, and I was amazed to discover that they in fact had challenges. Their personalities contradicted their positions, and I began to witness character deficits and personality quirks. They had insecurities and often had reactions that were born of those insecurities. With close examination, they were similar to my family. The difference was what they paid attention to. We were all about survival, they were all about definition. Neither group exercised true transitional thought.

Both families were attending to journeys of discovery. The journeys were different, yet similar. The people were the same; universal weaknesses were obvious. It was as if each needed a prescription for solutions to separate sets of challenges.

And So Goes Life

The pitcher sets,
he eyes the plate,
a stare of boastful hate.

I know that look,
that arrogant air,
that says I will be great.

His ego riding on a ball,
that hurtles
through the space.

For after all
he is their best;
he is their pitching ace.

He has to throw
his power pitch,
to beat you with his heat.

Lessons from the Trials of Life

To set you down,
a humbled form,
who has failed to do the feat.

His game is psych,
his intent to crush,
your fragile timid mind.

It's more than just
a pitch to him,
superiority his find.

My mind made up,
I set myself,
I dig in at the plate.

I drop my weight
and tense my arms,
more speed to generate.

I know he'll throw
his ego pitch,
I see it in his eyes.

And when he does,
I'll take it out,
So "come on, let her fly."

Carl Rice

He cocks his arm
and rips it down,
I lunge as in a dream.

I'm prepared to hear
the crack, the cheering,
and the screams.

Too late, I see a different spin,
not the missile
I had thought.

I'm out in front,
my timing's gone,
a swing without a swat.

Could I have judged
his facial ware,
have pondered too much his nerve?

Too late I know
indeed I have.
The bastard threw a curve.

And so it goes
in life's big game,
you try to press your fate.

Lessons from the Trials of Life

You make your choice,
and cast your lot,
with assuredness and faith.

But all your plans,
and most of your schemes,
are fruitless and contrite.

You play by chance
and when you guess the pitch,
sometimes it's just not right.

Shush

7

Confusing me is easy, as it is with most that look for truth. Truth is shrouded by circumstance. The very moment that I think I have it figured out I am given a new set of rules. The search had led me away from my family and into another. The standards were different; the resources were immense; the opportunity was not corrupted by survival; yet, the results were the same.

Human weakness punctuated by negativity was as challenging here as with my family. Great and large people had moments of weakness and were less than their station would allow. I was confused

Lessons from the Trials of Life

and could not find the trust to deal with the world. How do we move forward? My parents moved through the days the best they could in spite of having little and needing to give all to their children. My new connection moved forward with little regard for their luck and tried to get more while investing less.

What was the great task that life directed? It couldn't be simply survival. Our prefrontal brain makes it impossible to believe that survival is all this is about. There are too many poignant introductions, too many emotional variables, and too much recollection for me to believe the tired old axiom that primal needs are all there are. I have always suspected there was a reason for this existence, a task to accomplish, a lesson to learn, or a bill to pay. I discovered a word that was so loosely used that its definition actually caused a conflict with Darwinian principles.

What is this word love? Is there a logical definition that is not tainted by greed and lust? Does it really exist outside the confines of a deity? Can we expect to find it in our lives and if we find it, will we recognize it as more than a fleeting specter? It is strange how people run through their lives oblivious to the fact that breath is meaningless without an object. Try to find love and try not to run by it while you are busy pursuing its existence.

When you can define the word with any constant accuracy, how do you find it and how can you associate it with your life? " I love you," can be the meanest lie or the greatest compliment that one human can say to another.

There might be a Difference between love and respect!

Ode to L

I can't wait to love you
but you should take your time.
 I can offer you a score,
I'll give you love sublime.

I'll most likely hold you tight
and feel your warm sweet breath.
I'll want and need you more each day
and so until my death.

I'll live to love your everything,
your body, mind, and soul.
My love will give your heart a place to hide,
a place to call its home.

I'll dread my death
for it may be the end for you and me,
but more I dread the march of time
that takes your faith from me.

Lessons from the Trials of Life

When in my youth,
I laughed at time,
I felt days and nights
were friends.

I am still strong
but stubborn pains
remind me that a warrior
I have been.

I must face the creeping truth,
time's not a friend of mine.
And you should know I'm more than used,
my body's not a shrine.

I fear when seen in morning's light
when shadows can't erase,
the truth will take you from my side
and love might lose the race.

I dread the change that happens
to the host without good sense,
who tries to stay ahead of time
to keep his love intense.

The ecstasy of love well spent
when spent on keeping up,
can turn a king into a troll
whose need consumes all love.

Carl Rice

The object, of his love most dear,
will a servant be.
She might be chastened and lose her love
for a jealous King.

Please love me now,
and love me pure,
and love me
'til I'm spent.

But let's stay free
to give and get
all pleasure
and content.

Judge me kind when time's used up
and fires are but coals,
and know I'll give you everything
that's under my control.

Shush

Lessons from the Trials of Life

Carl Rice

8

I thought that I would develop the philosophical strength to deal with this pragmatically. Love was a word; service and contracts were the real way folks dealt with each other. Love was a limited resource that was to be vowed not understood. I looked back on my families and thought of the relationships that I had witnessed. I listened to people saying I love you each night before bed and each morning as they left for the day. They spent their energy investing in things and other people and came home to refuel for the futility of the following day. They chipped the paint off the gloss that was to be a loving family and took it back to the world to give it indiscriminately to folks that they sometimes didn't even like. They gave what they had till they had little and then they went home to the people that they "loved. " Is it any wonder that folks make love a lie.

Some folks might not really give a damn, but I think more often we do things without thinking of our motive and the consequences. I heard a guy discuss the fact that everyone looks at life through their own window. It seems realistic as we all are blessed or damned with a myriad of personal resolutions regarding our values. Psychologists have had a great time expounding on those facts and have boldly decided that those resolutions might affect how you deal with other folks.

Transactional analytics suggest that we treat others in a predetermined manner based on our perception of ourselves. My father convinced me that nurture was a driving force in the creations of those perceptions. I remember him saying that, be it animal or man, if you dominate there are only two choices: to roll on their backs in fear, or arise and fight. He claimed that neither was a clear picture of the nature of the animal; it was their version of what they had to do to survive! He also claimed that the act of domination was preconceived and often was a result of a lack of knowledge. I wonder then how much of human interaction is a lie based on survival on one side and manipulation on the other. What is real?

I have read and experienced enough that I too have developed a theory. There are basically two kinds of people: Givers and Takers.

Givers have developed a responsible, selfless personality. The pay it forward persona that is continually looking for a way to serve and support. They are slow to demand attention and quick to give credit. They are facilitators and fabric. They absorb responsibility and blame for failure, they are often the unsung heroes of the moment. They often are viewed as convenient but not essential.

They make good Linemen in football. I have decided that these people resolve their value as what they can do for others.

The Takers are more obvious personalities. They are the attention getters and in truth the advertisements for success. Theirs is the fame and attention that resonates when successes are accomplished. They often are given overt support for their efforts almost as if they deserve more support and adoration. They often also act like they alone are responsible for their success. These folks take and get till the moment is gone, then they continue to squeeze the tube of notoriety till the reason for the challenge is forgotten.

Both are further defined by nurture and thus are individualistic. Their joy or bitterness often is based on recognition and a result of their social environment. Thus, they are contributors based on their predilections and social expectations. They can both be frustrated by their own nature. Givers and Takers are consummate if uncomfortable team members.

Who Knew?

Beware the Woman who neuters her pets.
Her men aren't far behind.
She brings them home and scratches their ears,
she makes them food and pats their rear.
She keeps them close with kindness and deed,
she makes them think she supplies all needs.
She's loving and giving and kind.

Just wait till the urge to hunt or to quest
causes the brute to stray from the nest.
He thinks he is with her and still thinks he's free.
She thinks he is taken thus tame he must be.
She fixes adversity with a snip of the knife.
She demands the acceptance of her definition for life.

And when the beast is beaten and tame,
when the fires are quelled and soul is mundane.
She pats his head and goes off to the streets to
find a new pet to bring to her feet.

Be careful what you ask for

Shush

Carl Rice

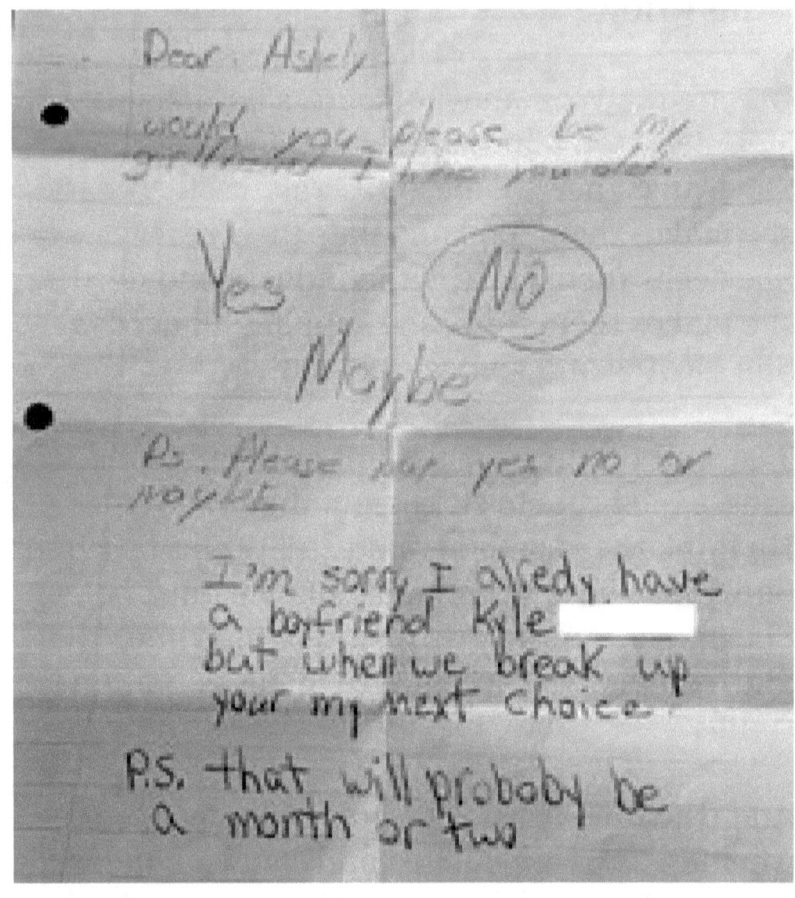

9

What in the world is love? Who in the world really loves us? Who do we really love? Can love and trust be symbiotic? These are the more obvious questions that have to be answered in order for us to create our emotional worlds. I have been told that I am loved by many humans on this trek through life, and to be honest, I have lightly attested to that fact on larcenous occasions to other folks. I have learned that the statement by itself is sinful. The comment, by itself, is most often used to coerce and control other individuals. I have also learned that the selfless consideration for an individual, love, is discovered through both joy and pain. Discovering that there is a consideration for a life that is not contingent on agreement with you is as important a transition as learning to breathe. Getting past "what's in it for me" is a necessity to generativity. I think it is also a necessity for finally learning to appreciate you.

I never really understood until I was a father and a Coach. When I finally felt it and reflected on relationships in my life I was embarrassed and ashamed. My recollections of deciding who loved me and who I loved had been a crap shoot and one that I got wrong a lot. I had been drawn to sensational people and had slowly moved away from substantial heroes.

I had been loved in the most lasting way by a family and a community that quietly affected my continued life. A mother and a Father who had little but gave all, individuals who taught me and graciously put up with my inconsistencies while reminding me that I had a chance, young friends and loves that saw in me what I did not, all helped me to tomorrow.

Love, the noun, is hard to define. Love seems like a contract more than fact. I will treat you with respect if you do what I want you to do seems to be the significant resolution of our time. What's in it for me might be a needed addition to the conditions.

Be careful when you profess a willingness to die

for someone's benefit, there are SOB's out there who actually think they deserve that effort. Is there a difference between love and respect?

You will make mistakes. You will likely pay for those mistakes. It is not the end of the road. You might think it is and you might decide that trying is not worth it. Why is that true?

Alone, The Day Within
(Commentary on jealousy, greed, and not knowing)

There he sat,
the room was stygian dark.
Alone within his realm he cringed
in the bellicose pit so stark.

I will not be afraid he said
there's an explanation for these straits.
The pit holds no forms or evil plots
to threaten so my way.

But God, each sound and each breathless wisp
of matter that passes by,
it shrinks his soul and annihilates
the calmness in his life.

He casts about with furtive gaze
to penetrate the wall,
but all he see's stygian black
no answers to his call.

Carl Rice

His fears resume relentless toils
to dominate his life.
His vivid dreams are sloshed about
and torn by doubt and fright.

None can see or hear his pain
as darkness answers calls.
He'll die inside unless he finds
the door within the wall.

Each person has a box like this
unfair as it may be.
A place of fear of endless strife
a place from which we flee.

Each person has a place like this;
we at times reserve the seat.
We take the time to lose all hope;
I pray it's not for me.

Sure as hell in time it came.
The reservation said,
"Attendance is required old boy, and by the way,
you're dead."

You don't need it all.

Shush

Lessons from the Trials of Life

10

Love, the verb, is hidden beneath a volume of personal inadequacies. This journey that we call life is a construct that is at once confusing and perilous. We're all trying to find our way to the other end with as little pain as possible. We stumble through relationships trying to sort out feelings that are selfish while evaluating the merits of those that we run into who are on a similar trek. We pass in the dark and rub against the realities of life proclaiming an intellect that is at once flawed and likely non existent. We cast about looking for truth and "love" and have no chance but for luck

to discover and embrace those enduring facets.
When one stops and recalls the moments in their lives that are poignant and real it is easy to affirm that the object of one's love is actually vested in innocence, and that we are ill equipped to embrace the object and the moment. We are often too ignorant to recognize and grasp the object and the instance for what they are a true blessing from God. We continue in emotional darkness begging for resolutions, looking for that fulfilling moment when our direction becomes clear and our prayers are answered. We so need the serenity that true love offers yet refuse to acknowledge the arenas that are presented. We live in a deep emotional fog that makes revelation an effort and a chance. Wisdom might be recognizing the epitome when it dances by your face in the persistent and enveloping fog that is an emotional life.

It is little wonder that mistakes are made! When do we quit trying? At times I think a majority just take their medicine and simply subside. They have little and can only choose to give what they have. The best definition of love was recited to me at a state student council convention. Love is wanting and working for the best, for an individual, that God could intend. The declaration doesn't suggest contracts or ownership, it does suggest selflessness. It seems noble and lofty. The definition doesn't however include the epitaph that should be included.

I remember when I was young and used to discuss with my friends topics that I absolutely knew nothing about. My Dad used to say it was like asking for financial advice from a bum on a backstreet in Denver. We came to lofty conclusions about right and wrong, good and bad, strength and weakness, and of course what and who we loved. Turns out none of us really knew what we were talking about.

I really didn't have a glimmer of understanding until I was blessed with my children. I had never experienced the true emotional journey that loving someone unconditionally presented. The joy that someone else's accomplishment could foster and the pain that their failure creates had never been a true reality. You can't cut and run if it is real. The epitaph "all who truly love you are blessed and doomed to share your journey," becomes a reality when we become committed to the welfare of another. The ability to act on that commitment is the result of a process. That process is the journey and a story.

Why The Hell
(Marriage and things I know nothing about)

He came into the valley
from where he could not say,
maybe fleeing from the strife in life
or living for the day.

Lessons from the Trials of Life

He camped below the northern ridge
a short way from the stream.
He spread his blankets, lit a fire
and drifted off to sleep.

He awakened in the morning
to peaceful harmony.
The birds that sang, the gurgling stream,
the whispering of the leaves,

all beckoned him toward
a spot he never thought he'd be,
a place to stay and call his home,
a place to live in peace.

He stayed there through the summer
and on into the fall.
He hunted and he rested there
and grew to love it all.

He journeyed through his newfound realm
exploring as he went.
He marveled at the beauty
and living was content.

He traveled south along the stream
to the canyon where it left,
and north along the lofty ridge
that overlooked the west.

But to the east he found a place
that filled his heart with dread,
upon a path well worn and stark
with short and measured tread.

It upward wound into the dark
no purpose to extol,
when all at once his progress blocked
by a cliff morose and cold.

It rose into the still night air
and seeming disappeared,
its width so great it filled the night
on all three sides it leered.

In his heart, he felt a dread
uncalled and so unnamed.
No reason could he kindle
as a motive for his scream.

Yet he gazed upon the brink
of the great foreboding face.
Retreat turned to panicked flight
from this dread filled place.

He'd not return to this dark path
and so he would not dwell
on why he felt the fear,
un-reason, and the hell.

Lessons from the Trials of Life

In time he forgot its presence there
and life it seemed so sweet,
all was good and pure and right,
no reason for retreat.

So he lived without regret
and passed from need and haste.
His comfort so consoled his soul
that trust his dread replaced.

Days turned into dreamy weeks
and weeks and months did fly.
The hunting wolf became the dog,
complacent did he lie.

Little did he understand
the smoke off to the west,
that burned with brands and spark filled air
toward his camp it pressed.

A raging force revealed itself
and scattered all before.
It drove all life before its surge
toward the east it roared.

He ran away as all life did
to escape this awful foe.
He was forced up the dark and dread filled path
that once before he'd strolled.

Carl Rice

Chased by imps and dreaded spires
he reached the cliff's cold face.
He knew that here he'd lose the fight
and his promise be erased.

Still he leaped upon the cold hard rock
and clambered up the face.
He fell and gathered all his might
and tried the feat again.

Twice, then thrice, and five, and six,
he struggled forth to find
that all his efforts bold and strong
were useless and contrite.

When all his strength and mental might
were finally expelled,
he turned to face the roaring fire
and hurried off from hell.

Why and if this chastened soul
could ever understand
the reason for his trap
and fate within a master plan.

He lived then died
and none can see the reason for this test.
His life all gone and promise to
with the fire from the west.

Lessons from the Trials of Life

But come next spring
with rain and snow
and fertile soil and warmth,
the trap will once again be set.

Some fool will call this home.

Shush

11

I became a Coach. The progression was not thrust on me; it seemed like a natural ascent into life. I was searching for validity, for meaning, for a family that would not disappoint me. I had forgotten the most important lessons and was in need of a revelation.

I first came in direct contact with "my own team" while attending college. I coached a bunch of ornery Hispanic kids in a youth basketball league. I was as bad a coach as they were basketball players, but for that short period in my life, and I hope in theirs, I discovered some meaning. The struggle was not about basketball, thank God, it was however about unfettered and real relationships. We became attached and committed to something. It didn't seem like it was ever about getting better at the sport. It was about learning to care more about each other and our efforts together than it was about our anger at being overlooked and disregarded.

We struggled with the embarrassment of entering into the competitive arena dressed in tattered t-shirts and worn out gym shoes. Our shorts were not matching; we were not good shooters; we didn't know fancy plays; and we were drubbed regularly at the beginning of the season. Our opponents had a number of obvious advantages and we continually supplied them with the greatest advantage of all. We felt they were better than us, and we helped them prove it.

The third game of the year, we were thrashed and failed to score a single point. Following the game, we huddled at the end of the gym and one little fellow proclaimed, in profane words, how much he hated basketball. The whole group, nine of the toughest little guys in the town, agreed. The team was all about disintegrating and to be truthful I had had enough. I couldn't come up with a speech that would console and cause them to continue. I was as embarrassed for them as they were for themselves, and to be truthful, I saw no way to help them. We slowly walked out of the Baptist

Church Gym, and when my thoroughly defeated little group was about to go through the door into the street, we were confronted by two parents. The parents of the team that had just drilled us, disparaged the way we looked and played. They actually said that it was ridiculous for us to be in the league. I forgot one of the important lessons my Father had taught me. The strength that it took to be gentle eluded me.

I went after the Upper Middle class Baptist fathers with both colorful condemnation and physical ire. The battle was short, and it was obvious to all that they were not suited for the type of confrontation that I had afforded them. My nine little impressionable and terrible basketball players were the only ones in the gymnasium that were supportive of my efforts. They were enough!

I was called in to visit with the town recreation director the following Monday and relieved of my coaching duties. I remember thinking that he was correct in his actions, and that it wasn't that bad anyway because no-one on the team wanted to continue. The acquiescent acceptance of his stance didn't change the fact that I was still angry. The fact that the deck was stacked against my little friends, and that everyone seemed to think it was ok, infuriated me. I felt like I was joining the "piling on" by not resisting, but I gritted my teeth and left.

Lessons from the Trials of Life

I came home after my last class to my humble castle. The front door to my old two room camper trailer on Fifth Street, was surrounded by nine little Hispanic kids, four Mothers and two Dads. They had a single demand, continue to coach the little fellows. I explained that I knew little about basketball and even less about accepting the obvious indiscretion of the recreation league and its privileged members. I told them that I was not apt to act properly if the injustice continued. They said that was good, they left me two pans of homemade enchiladas, and said they would take care of the rest. The following morning I was reinstated. We finished the season and actually became competitive. We didn't play better basketball, but we were so physical that teams struggled to score.

I regularly stepped out of my trailer to go to morning classes to find delicious pans of authentic Mexican Food setting on my front step. The families had little but they gave what they had!

I still think of those nine boys, and to be honest, that memory has helped drive me throughout my private and professional life. They supplied me a reason to climb outside of my own insecurities and gave me the need to press for someone else's benefit. They represented the first group in my life that I needed to advocate for, to provide resources to, and to prepare to eventually be on their own. I didn't realize it but they became my first extraneous family. I hated it when the season was over and I no longer met with them. I had yet to learn that caring for someone meant that you might eventually have to let them go.

The Cave

The Shaman sat in the dim lit hole that acted as a door to the stark rock wall that blocked the way for all that ventured forth.

"What brings you here," he questioned me as I peered into the dark; "are you looking for a path within that leads you back to earth?" It stinks in here I answered back and its dark beyond belief. "Is it safe within or does this passage lead to grief?" I fear the dark for within its grip all reason leaves my skull and every little chance I take seems to burden so my soul.

The wise old man just smiled back at the novice he did see. His old grey eyes looked through my head to a heart that seemed diseased. "You know the path within this cave may lead you to a dream, it could be peace, it could be wealth, it could be all you need."

"Yet you fear to enter in for the path is not well made, you fear the dark and wraiths of life whose tolls you have not paid. This gate from air to mother earth, may house the imps of hell. You cannot move, you're frozen stiff, you might not break the spell. Fear stops your limbs from moving forth and ends your needed quest. You might lose your mind and to your soul in this empty pit of death. "

"I see you might refuse the chance to enter here by me. I know your choice is harried by these dangers you perceive. Once inside the dread might turn you white with fear for the maize of paths that lead away, confuse the steadfast clear. Many a path leads to hell and few to lifelong peace. It is understood if you cannot move to take a chance with me. I respect the careful way in which your choice is made for very few can enter here and embrace the stay. "

"On the other hand I have witnessed the plight of those who fear. They stand real still and simply play the hand that they are dealt. They would like to change, to walk or run toward a better day but all paths are refuted for the dangers they might have. No matter for the pain endured by standing ever still and the minutes lost in terrors grip that seems so close to hell. The feet and mind are both numbed and blind to the essence of a chance to change the life of a sickened soul by striking on a path. "

"The path that you might take with me may not be where you thought. It could be hard, it could be dark, and I could get you lost. I promise though to stay with you and help you through your fear. I'll take your hand and give you strength you'll always know I'm near. For out of sight my soul will guide you through this stark dark cave, and within my power I'll help you to the treasures that you crave.

I will lift you up and bid you go when our journeys through, for life within this cave of mine is only for a few. So make a choice, decide your fate, jump or just turn back! My cave awaits selected souls who choose to take a chance."

The old man smiled and turned away; he gave me not a glance. I guess he saw no light in me that said, *I'd take the chance*. Well now I sit at that cave's door and wait for wary souls that venture here, with stricken hearts that wonder where to go. I offer them the same slim chance that was given me before, the chance to go beyond their fear with the keeper of the door.

Shush

12

A certain power is afforded to souls that learn the truth. The truth is not about the world; it is about themselves. The world is a canvas of sorts that might be impossible to change, in merit, but whose surface can be affected. Man's singular efforts leave small marks, man's collective efforts evolve on the surface like a vibrant and beautiful painting, or a nasty scar.

The creation that speaks of man's existence is a complicated and motile concept. What is a good life? Is it accumulations of wealth and recognition, is it creating a widget, is it being philosophically adept, is it being faithful and spiritual, is it being an effective manager of resources, or might it be being a giver?

The act of loving is as complicated as ascertaining the Good Life. How do you labor to affectively and effectively love someone? Do you provide physical resources, do you pressure them to accept your determinations of truth, do you teach about strength, courage, and honor, do you leave them to discover for themselves?

Our lives might need to exhibit nothing more than loyalty. I had a huge great dog. He adored me and grew to be obedient and remarkably forgiving. He provided me with adoration, protection, and company. He was the same if I was angry or thrilled. He wanted to be with me when I was emotionally spent and when I was vibrant. I thought he was the epitome of love. He mourned so when I was gone; he wouldn't eat; he paced and worried. I wandered if I was not there, would he be able to go on?

I also remember a horse that I partnered with while I was young. We traveled and made money together; I fed him and he served me, but I can honestly say I never owned him. He was big, strong, and idiosyncratic. He did his job and was loyal to a point. He did his job as long as you treated him in an accepted way. If you strayed, he rebelled. His was not unconditional adoration, and his rebellions were often painful. I knew he trusted in me as he accepted his role in our lives. I grew to think he loved me because I accepted his peculiar nature.

I am sure neither of these beasts spent a lot of time thinking and planning an emotional regimen. I, in fact, am the one who did the reflecting. I have met a lot of folks in my life that are very similar to those animals. Reflection and a decision are absent in their interactive reality. They seem in one case to be ordained to loyalty and in the other to a partnership based on performance.

Is love either of these conditions, or is it in fact the decision that comes from reflection? When once it is proclaimed does it require consummate effort? Does it require a cognitive connection? Is respect the final element in love? Just think how difficult that cognitive connection would be, if a soul is internally ignorant.

A loving, giving model might be necessary for the proliferation of this species. Our survival is so dependent on love based on a cognitive realistic connection. We in turn seem more selfish than ever. Have we lost the ability to love the mother Earth, and each other? Do we so demand credit and adoration that we simply will not contribute without fame?

I want my biological children and my surrogates to have prolific lives. I want them to be strong in character, thoughtful, compassionate, courageous, and loving. I also want them to be wary enough as to not be victims. I remember a conversation with a trusted colleague regarding what we taught our children. The discussion about honesty and integrity was examined based on what the world around them embraced. We wondered if we at times erred in the attempt to make good kids bastions of integrity when they had to venture into a society that rewarded the opposite. Do we make them potential victims? The prolific citizen might be the individual that can evaluate personal, social, and professional variables. The reaction then would be tailored to that evaluation. What if life is more clinical than we would like to admit?

    I have learned that the act of loving requires us to arise from disasters and attend to our real purposes to support our intended. We actually own nothing; not the land, not the water, not the air, and certainly not other people. Is it not ironic that most of our efforts are spent in acquisition and too little is spent in giving.

The Epic Battle

Not long ago nor far removed
beneath a sodden sky of gloom
the once great King, a broken man
must accept his coming doom.

His head is bowed, his bloodied brow
they reveal a broken heart,
there is nothing left of the warrior soul
that defended home and hearth.

His weapons strewn about him on the ground,
his armor bent and hacked.
His once steel eyes now downward turned
his fate a certain fact.

His enemies, the demons of the rock,
all celebrate his certain fate.
What chance has he against their press
against the kingdom's gate?

With derisive laughs, victory is theirs,
his army has no cause.
The flag is down, the champion crushed
and the end is what they sought.

Theirs is the power, the awesome power,
of fate and hate and wrong.
No living soul, be it man or King,
can resist their surge for long.

But did they celebrate too soon?
Upon the rock beneath the gloom a figure stirs
      anew.
A broken frame, with bloodied brow,
arises from his doom.

Carl Rice

He will not yield his kingdom's gates,
his people he'll not fail,
he must find a way to stand and fight,
his will may yet prevail.

He lifts his sword, he finds his shield,
he forces himself erect.
He stands alone with heart and soul
as of a king you might expect.

He raises his fist, his bloodied fist,
he knows that he must try.
To hell with fear and existence dear,
he gives forth his battle cry!!

Some will deny that this fight exists
that this battle must be fought.
They think that men are consigned by fate
and righteous struggle is for naught.

The haggard soul that is The King,
he knows that men are as they choose.
They may live their life with scuttled dreams,
and, in the end, will lose.

Or they may see and challenge forth
the wrong that fills this earth,
and fight the press that hurries death
and have another birth.

Lessons from the Trials of Life

For heroes, friend, I've heard it said
that life in death does hide
for those of us who dare to fight
and not for those that hide.

Each person lives whatever life
that God has given them.
With certain truth, each human will attend
and then will end.

They struggle forth through life's rich text
they bend and some may fail,
but be assured the blame for you
resides in you and not in some travail.

Shush

13

Good and evil plants exist in all of us. The ones that grow are the ones that we water. I believe in the potential of the human existence and deep down I know that when we ignore kindness and choose despotic methods to control our sisters and brothers we lose their potential. We actually encourage divisiveness. The environment becomes personally competitive. We look at ridiculous personal variables and lose our significant attention to the greater cause. We become weaker.

I paid a lot of money in university studies to discover that the father of modern sociology,

Lessons from the Trials of Life

Durkheim, claims that we are moral to the point that we are social. My father put it in a distinctively different way when he asked, "Do you know what the white stuff in chicken shit is?" He would then stated, with a wry smile, "that is chicken shit too. " His point, you are who you hang with, and if you choose poorly you are without defense.

I feel we can be moral in spite of being social. I believe we make it more difficult by our social choices. We are all strung together by a universal ethic or model. I think one can recognize right and wrong when internally attentive. You have been blessed. Realize that your life has consequence on this earth. Think how many you touch with your decisions. I realize that much of the time we concentrate on the monster, the far removed imaginary machine. The truth is — the real struggle rages in the individual. We cannot compete without, until we quiet the demons within. Ethics doesn't just happen, it is a chosen practice.

"The good of the many outweighs the needs of the one. " Thank you Spock! If this is true, is it confined to emergencies? Is it a lifelong doctrine if we are to survive? I know it is antithetical to the great capitalists that directed my early life, but I also know that their wealth was contingent on the physical efforts of numerous less blessed working souls.

When we lie in state at the end of our earthly existence, does the capitalist have a better chance at glory? Maybe we are all of the same meat.

What the hell is an act of random love? Is it a decision or is it simply an innocent act that enhances existence? Who really knows? When is killing another person or animal an act of valor and when is it a crime?

Maybe it is all determined by social perspective. That's a scary thought!

Social perspectives can be institutionally controlled. Educational systems, political systems, and entertainment are examples of elements that control mass perspectives. Our morality, according to Durkeim, thus is programmed by external institutions. We often accept, as truth, resolutes that are not internally accurate. When do we kill? Is it noble to kill for competitive, religious, or political reasons? Are drug crimes and sexual deviance worse than usury? Are we absolved of individual responsibility for heinous acts if we perform them under the guise of our institutionally directed morality? Soldiers, preachers, lawyers, teachers, law enforcement, and bankers, are some of those constituents. Maybe Kipling had it right when he said you only kill to eat or to keep from being eaten! Maybe my Dad was right when he said that we all lose when we give away the right and responsibility to determine our moral definition.

I am confounded by the lack of cognitive participation that humans display. We have a marvelous ability to question. We have the ability to solve problems through experimentation and adaptations that allow us to expose realities and yet we allow ourselves to be conditioned like lab animals. The truth is that most are too lazy to think. We are also too selfish to accept that others have internal directives for survival. Plato's Cave might be real!

I've spent most of my life trying to escape the obvious and to find a possibility.

I've been assigned many names mostly based on my looks or performance and by what I can provide for the people who are naming. I am struck by the fact that most of the folks who do this neither know or care who you might be. I am also struck by the observation that when their need for you is lessened that meaningful contact evaporates. I think most folks are the same in this way; it is a figment of a shallow species.

I have tried to live up to many of those shallow and inaccurate definitions. To my ultimate demise, I have been a son, a brother, a friend, a lover. I have been embraced and erased, accepted and rejected, found and lost, bought and given away. I have been helped and used, paid for and sued, served and abused, all in the effort to get to you.

The effort to find you, and to embrace you, and to stay with you, have led me down numerous paths. The journey has been an adventure and the result has been the creation of a complex soul. Results have been a mix of satisfaction and pride, to pain and shame. I have become gifted in saying what should be said, and I can recognize what others need and in a lot of cases provide those needs. I am accepted in professional circles and have had my share of notoriety. I have been a darling for a moment and a clown for eternity. I have had friends and enemies I've been here and there, but I haven't been able to get to you.

I have lived a while and have had the opportunity to reflect on my existence. I am not as confused as I once was by this twisted journey. I can see a bit more clearly the object that I crave. The new clarity is a concerning element in my continuing and final quest. I am proceeding with less time and fewer tools than ever in my life. Gone are the instances when opportunity jogged in and out my life, times when you presented yourself unselfishly to me and then drifted aimlessly away. I didn't or wouldn't recognize a need and thus the embrace was ill expressed. I languish now with the realization that I might have missed my chance to be with you.

I arise and prepare for each day, the boring procedures that pronounce a meaningless existence, to an end of no particular consequence. Each day seems an interruption to efforts that I should be making towards an end with you. I think and with halfhearted effort try to place myself. I'm reserved and am lacking in resolve. I prepare myself for accepting that I will not find you.

Energy and vision are commodities that can invest in hope. Time is the quotient that divides them both. I'll try to carry on for the sake of those who need my efforts. I can give what I have until what I have is gone. Maybe then, when all is done and time is lost and hope doesn't matter, I will finally find you.

The greatest pain that I have endured in my life has occurred when I allowed myself to attach to other humans. To say I love you and mean it, to act for the benefit and needs of that love, means you expose your very soul to the possibility of agony.

I suspect that a meaningful life is dependent on the acceptance of that danger. The hunger for closeness and the need for relationships that are defined by trust and vulnerability are necessary but they do allow people the ability to hurt you.
I have outlived most of the people that have that ability. The ones that are left are carrying on!

Twixt Evanston and You
(essay on choosing life)

A trip I need to calm my mind
and occupy my life.
The family's gone, so I've no home
to hold my heart at night.

Carl Rice

Oh, what to do and where to go,
I can't believe this trial,
it's like a pain that will not leave,
not even with denial.

A choice to make twixt fear and need
it seems a simple task,
A needless jaunt or mindless press
toward uncertain acts.

Behind the wheel with grit and grind
I forge into the night,
a press toward another place,
a journey to the light.

I'm lost, though all I know
is at my beck and call,
so I've a choice to go to you
or just move until I fall.

You frighten me, you do not care,
with you I'm not my own.
I flee from you
more than the fear of being here alone.

Up north I find a place
where no one wants to go,
it sits upon a barren plain
and has no warmth I know.

Lessons from the Trials of Life

But it's far away from where I am
and so I'll head that way,
to spend this time of joyous tides
to waste these endless days.

It sits a distance from the road
upon a lonely hill,
a plastic place that gets its life
from travelers not thrills.

In a gnarly hut that's called an Inn,
a room with number 8,
a place to hide for six long days
in a God forsaken state.

The choice I made to stay away
at least it was my plan:
I drove all night to flee from you
and stayed in Evanston.

My brother drilled for oil
up there back in '95,
I knew before I journeyed north
it's no place to be alive.

I thought about the nights I spent
and those listless endless days,
the thoughts of you that cursed my mind
in every poignant way.

Carl Rice

The bitter cold that pressed the earth
and howling wind that blew.
I hated every minute there
but it was far away from you.

When days had passed, I arrived back home
to see that things had changed.
No place could ever be my home,
nothing was the same.

Alone at night I often think
about those listless nights,
my mind once more relives
the hell of that endless mental flight.

The choice again resounds within
I must choose just what to do,
with you to stay or drive away,
it's Evanston or you!

As time goes by I'll find the need
to take a trip again,
a place away though I might say
please not like Evanston.

Shush

14

I was raised with an understanding that life might be a transient reality. The difficulty that pronounced our early life, though innocuous when you were in the moment, suggested that there had to be something better down the road. I couldn't understand how some seemed so blessed while we were without. My family didn't take the time to cry for help, we were too busy existing. I knew, however, that my parents rued the fact that they were in a paradox. They had bigger dreams than reality would allow. No money, too little time, and too much responsibility, made for poignant regrets. The opportunity for bitterness was obvious but never a central motive.

When we were young, Mom decided we needed religion. We started going to a little country church called the Burlington Gospel Chapel. The church was small in membership, and the preacher was a successful farmer who was adept at farming corn and souls. Ben, the preacher, was a substantial man with a huge presence. The congregation was a combination of farmers, small town business families, local educators, and comfortable retired folks. All were common and authentic people, who as a community were a pivotal and powerful force in my young life.

I am sure we were on Ben's radar as needing his attention. He was inordinately interested in this brood that started showing up for Sunday School and Church. We were in regular attendance and usually without my Dad. He often had to work for the farm that employed him. Dad did support Mom's decision to attend to our spiritual needs and often discussed his formative years revealing that his family had been pillars in the church where he was raised.

I can remember that Ben thought Dad was "a problem" in the needed conversion of his family. He visited with Mom, following church one Sunday. Ben was invited to supper the following Tuesday. My brothers and I looked at each other with what might be considered latent apprehension. I had worked for Ben on his farm and realized that he employed me out of pity for our financial situation. I spent a lot of time killing weeds in the lengthy windbreak at his farm. His wife, a lovely human, always fed me lunch and made me snacks, so I spent some time in what I thought was his castle. They had beautiful furniture, carpeted floors, a separate dining room, a washer and a dryer, and a television! I could not believe that people actually lived with those luxuries.

Ben lived in a mansion that was always clean and supplied with everything that a person could wish for. He was coming to our house for a meal; I wondered what the heck mom was thinking. She must have been desperate. I wondered if she actually thought we were that savage. Whatever the motive, Tuesday arrived. Mom started preparing the meal very early, and I remember that she was actually cooking a variety of food groups. She cooked fried chicken, potatoes and gravy; she baked bread and a cake with chocolate frosting. She had covered our old punished table with her only table cloth. She got out the best dishes that we had and set the table. I knew she was trying to show her best because few of the plates were chipped and the cups mostly matched.

Ben was punctual! He arrived precisely at 6:30 and walked into our one room kitchen/dining room/living room. The floors had been scrubbed using a bucket and a mop, they were devoid of shoes, clothes, and extraordinary mess. Mom had even done her best to disguise the condition of our living room couch and Dad's Chair. We had scrounged dining chairs for everyone. Three different styles of chairs that were placed almost against each other surrounded the pedestal that we referred to as a table. Mom was ready!

We politely assembled and entered into uncomfortable conversation with our guest as my mother attempted to excuse my father's tardiness. We had been forced to put on shirts and shoes and we had been forewarned regarding manners. Our wait was rewarded after what seemed like an eternity of graciousness. Dad's old pickup growled to stop in the front of the house and he came in the front door. He had been cleaning out a grain bin with a scoop shovel and was caked from head to toe with grain dust. He was obviously fatigued but tried to put up a cheerful and hospitable front. He went into the wash room and did his best to remove the grime from what had been a difficult afternoon. He came to the table where we had all assembled and took his place in the chair at the head.

What transpired immediately following that presentation has stayed forever in mind. The resolution that it prompted has either corrupted or blessed my existence on this earth. Dad sat down at the table and my mom brought what we thought was a feast. She sat beside Dad and he took the platter of chicken, he selected the gizzard, which

Lessons from the Trials of Life

he always did, along with a leg, he then handed the chicken to Ben. Ben didn't take the chicken! He, instead, indignantly cleared his throat and asked: "Don't you pray before you eat?"

The room became silent. Ben was staring directly at my father, and my father, who was not violent but lived with a conviction, was eyeballing him. The tension was real if not unnecessary. I actually wondered if Dad was going to grab Ben and drag him from the house. I took care of the prayer, I silently asked that this end. Following a caesura, the tension was broken when Dad said slowly, "We don't have to pray, Momma is a good cook!"

The meal continued with a profound discomfort. The tension was never alleviated, and when Ben left there was genuine relief. We finished the chicken after mom and dad retreated to the bedroom . We didn't realize that anything was wrong until Dad went outside in the dark and Mom went to the bathroom with tears in her eyes.

I was puzzled by the ordeal. Why would something as simple as taking chicken from a plate lead to a disagreement between two decent men? My Dad and Ben were really quite different. One worked, the other managed; one was wealthy while the other was economically challenged; one talked for a living, the other spoke in measured tones, one pressured others to accept his way of thinking while the other encouraged personal conviction. I could see that disagreement might be a reality. I thought at length about this failed opportunity for mother to coordinate efforts for her sons and the resulting conflict. I wondered what would happen should they meet later.

I was young and even then I had the suspicion that what had happened represented something way bigger than the obvious. I to realized that Ben and my Dad had similarities. Both were courageous and both convicted by the need to be honest. Both cared deeply for their children. Dad loved us in an obvious fashion and Ben, to his credit, loved his flock. Both were faithful, yet responded in different ways. Yet here they were at a seeming loggerhead over chicken. Seemed to me like the argument, over whether to pray for the chicken, might not be necessary. I also thought they needed to take a long ride together.

Ben and Mom were the first to establish my spiritual need and also the first to expose idiosyncrasies that challenged the Simple Message. Formative individuals, from my parents, to old time preachers, mothers of high school friends, friends, teachers and coaches, as well as significant caregivers, have presented modeling for my personal beliefs. Each of these well meaning people shared their doctrines and have dramatically affected me. They have all been adept at explaining at length what I should believe and conversely what I should condemn. The last part of that calculation has always confounded me. I have never been able to condemn people for what they really believe. I have learned however that saying you believe and truly believing might not be a reality. Life tests supposition and resolve! The result should be a personal opus, a tiny but enduring thread in the tapestry that is human identity. I don't think I am equipped to make the determination of that reality for other folks.

Ben judged my father's motives because he didn't symbolically pray over a tray of chicken. He determined that my father might not have spiritual substance and as a result needed to be led to his light. He had pre-concluded then reinforced that conclusion by applying faulty reasoning, reasoning that was based on a vastly inaccurate set of perceptions.

I have witnessed laws that are made and enforced because folks are different. The Crusades allowed Europeans to kill innocent people because their idea of God was different than the Saxons; the Salem Witch Trials occurred from fear and ignorance, the crux of which was a difference in perceptions; millions have been killed for either Economic, religious, or Political differences. I could go on, but suffice to say that in each of these iniquities, judgment is made without understanding the others condition and motives. We become so caught in our sanctity and greed that we have to destroy anything that might challenge. We ignore justice and dignity while maligning the message.

Introspect is threatening but necessary for the evaluation and eventual consolidation of our spiritual definition. I don't believe we have that identity until we realize that our walk is truly ours. We should strive to dignify the individuals search for faith and reality. The view is always different.

The Tinkling of Kimberly's Bell: The Final Search

The dark descends. The crispness of the evening air hints at another savagely cold December night. The fragrance of the burning Aspen logs and the twinkling of newly hung Christmas lights lure the frost bitten traveler toward the warm and vibrant havens lining the innocent street of the little mountain village. Within the confines of the cottages voices waft in merriment and fall in subdued fashion oblivious to the threatening conditions beyond their safe yet confining walls. The souls within are happy and far from need yet quite isolated from each other. They are very far away from the promise of severity that lurks beyond their window panes.

Outside, a lonely traveler emerges from the dusk beneath the bright light of a newly installed street light. His gait is stiff and labored and there is a hint of malady hiding in his joints. With effort he moves from one shadow to the next and passes up the street toward its apex. The snow makes a crackling noise as his worn boots tread onward toward his unsure destiny.

Darkness settles on the little mountain town. Silence envelopes the shops and street doors close with finality as the traffic subsides to nothingness. The stage is set, the harsh beauty of a mountain night, its bitter cold, the silent lesson of life and survival, the quaint little mountain town with twinkling lights and muted people, between the two a stranger of unknown quality. At stake a life of any sort and the answer to the question. What Matters?

Three blocks from main-street, two blocks from the only traffic light, and about a hundred yards from the last thriving business in town a tiny calico kitten prances through the night. It stops to glare at shadows and occasionally swats flakes of hoar frost dripping from the night sky. The frail animal dips and dives, it rolls and plays in sequences of fanatic behaviors oblivious to the promise of natural cruelty surrounding her.

Dusk turns to dark and with it a settling cold that solidifies liquid and slows the flesh. The heavy air seems to mandate silence as it presses the earth and long deep silence prevails. It prevails except for a frail yet clarion sound that escaped the confines of the trash cans behind the Big Bear cafe and lounge. It was a high and faint note yet clear and precise. It bore a certain beauty to the beholder but it seemed out of place and in definite danger. It was the tinkle of the tiny bell on the kitten's collar.

With a sudden start the small animal exited the trash cans and emulating a feline jet shot across the alley and into the shadows surrounding an old and tattered awning that had once been attached to the back of Kline's Mercantile. Spooked and frightened the kitten crouched within the recesses of the shadows and inspected the form hovering above the apparatus that had been its former playground. A wraith of sorts, lingered above the smaller of the two cans. The apparition leaned against the wall while studying the contents. It then went to one knee and with haste born of desperate need started pawing through the trash. Uttering A small squeal of delight the wraith consumed two half eaten breasts of chicken that were plucked from the depths of the can. The meal continued with Texas Toast that some diner hours before had discarded because of its sandy texture. He lingered hoping that something else remained in his newfound lunch pail. He scratched and dug at the entrails of the can and his tattered garments danced as if tied to the beat of a sprightly Irish anthem. The movement was more than the kitten could stand. She charged out of shadows with a resounding tinkle and launched herself at the remnants that had once been the sleeve of a nylon windbreaker.

With a grunt of surprise the scavenger jumped to

his feet and snatched his arm upward as if to avoid the fangs of a predator. The kitten clung some six feet off the ground, claws attached to the strands of the wraiths sleeve. Screaming with fear the man flapped his arm like a bird taking to the wing, the kitten dislodged and projected into the shadows from which she had come and was silent. Eyes still wide with fear, the man stood and the light from the dishwasher's throne revealed a gaunt bearded face. He stared through eyes that bore into the dark, large round eyes that had seen much and much of what he had seen had been cause for pain. In answer to his furtive stare a silent form caught his eye and a small whimper called his attention to the tiny form huddled against the wall of the old building. With measured step he approached the form and hunkered over a calico kitten with a small silver bell around its neck. He knelt and with trembling hands retrieved the tiny form. He scrutinized it with those hard round eyes and as he did tears escaped the confines of the folds surrounding them. A remorseful groan escaped him, he was ashamed. He had struggled long to live, so consumed with the effort that he had forgotten moments when finding food and fending off danger were not the only requirements for life. He sobbed praying he had not killed the fragile thing in his hands.

He cuddled the kitten to his body holding it as if proximity to his heart would hasten its revival.

He leaned his back against the wall and slowly slid to the frigid ground. He sat, the kitten lying on his chest, and he tumbled inwardly. He remembered that before he had been a bright somewhat intimidating youth. It had seemed he was the chosen of his species: the strongest, the swiftest, and the one who would use wisdom to cudgel the wrongs of the world. He had looked forward to each morning and had reveled in each night. His had been the perpetual joy of life, and then he was introduced to death. The introduction had started with boot-camp and had ended in a muddy trench halfway around the world.

Now he was tired. The battles of the war had taken his warmth and the struggles of continued life had taken his resolve. It seemed as if the tiny form lying on his chest was the final defeat. The cold bore down on his forlorn form. It numbed his limbs and his mind. It was preparing him for his final chapter, the last few lines in the essay of his life. This wandering soul had paid too horrible a price for his simple needs. Born to a town and a country, he had been taught ideals of life, he had believed in beauty and truth. Reality, a cold ruthless suitor had beaten him. He was home again but his life would pass as it began, a byline of little note in a paper read by few.

Ideals can still be fueled by these facts. A bell was heard the morning he was found. A faint and clarion song with high and beautiful notes had

Lessons from the Trials of Life

beckoned to early morning passers by. The object of his final guilt had lived! No-doubt warmed by the fading fire of his soul, its existence a testimony to the gentler life, the song of laughter and the simple beauty that is a child's love. Kimberly, her bell intact would be returned to the three year old who loved her, a gift from the soul of a forgotten man who in death had given life, a gift to innocence and love and maybe the only testimony that matters.

Shush

Carl Rice

15

I knew nothing about myself until I had children. I had been living a lie! I had a lifetime of experience and was still devoid of wisdom and understanding. I didn't know myself, and I was about to learn that I was not ready for my biggest test. The experience is how God humbles us! I have never felt as vulnerable as when I was faced with the need to say the right thing or do the perfect thing to help my kids to a more prolific life. The pure motivation to guide and intercede for your creation is the greatest test of your merit. The fact that you dare not fail and the realization that you hold complete responsibility for that soul gives you more than pause. It is the most virulent test of your path.

My children are conglomerations of their mother and me. They represent the very best of both of us, and at times, exhibit the very worst of our dwindled definition. It is impossible for them to surprise me with actions that I have not witnessed in both of their parents. They move through our lives like a simultaneous reflection, they grow too fast and adjust in an uncontrolled fashion.

The impossibility of programming their existence becomes a reality before they are through their baby clothes. The remainder of their childhood is a blur and your only affect is to be the best model that you can be. I often laugh at people who have the nerve to think that they have directed their children to goodness or faithfulness or opportunity. Truth, goodness, and faithfulness can be transient and might depend on circumstance as much as reality. The celebration for that adoption is also transient.

The greatest test of parenthood becomes a question. Where do you go when things get tough? When kids challenge predetermined values or simply fail to apply their truths. Do you disappear and if you don't, do you intervene and become the savior? I have learned that no one really knows what to do. The correct response is not always

correct. The fact that behavioral determinations control responses and results in huge numbers of variables for the actor. When the variables of the savior are added in there is no way to predict what proper response is. I can see why a lot of species lays their eggs and then gets the hell out of there.
I won't pretend to know the answers. I do know that real love won't let you quit trying. I also suspect that children figure love out based on the fact that people who love them show up! I had a friend who owned a huge and profitable apple orchard. I purchased a home that had a little patch of apple trees on it, and I questioned him about how to trim the trees. He told me that apple trees were quite forgiving. He said if you toil to give them water and nutrients and keep the suckers out of them they will produce good fruit. My experience with children is the same. Take care of them and keep the suckers away and they will respond! In both cases the greatest sin is to ignore and quit trying.

Thank You Mom and Dad!!

A Legacy

Time has the light of day,
begun to steal from me.
The beauties of the earth, they fade,
and but faintly can I see.

Lessons from the Trials of Life

The dusk, it robs my sight
and hastens forth a fear,
that soon the long and stormy night
will bring a time of tears.

I hastily prepare my house
for the coming gloom.
I gather in my pressing needs
before the pending doom.

There is a chance before the press
to see the last bright ray,
the softest light most brilliant shone,
the final light of day.

I'll keep that light within my mind
as a shield from the fright,
which most certainly will pervade
my thoughts in the dark and mournful night.

And if by chance, by certain chance,
I prevail within the dark
and arrive at dawn a selfless man
to seek another start.

I'll take that ray of bygone hours,
that small but brilliant light,
and give it to someone of need
who must face their darkest night.

Shush

Carl Rice

Our one chance

Lessons from the Trials of Life

Invisibility

I thought I knew a guy.
He was blunt and sure.
He was funny when he wanted.
He could be powerful or gentle.

He was talented and needy
in the very same sentence.
He was fun to be around
and terrible to refuel.

He was the very definition of confusing.
Hell, he didn't even know himself!!!

About the Author

Carl Rice is a retired teacher, coach, and principal who guided many youth throughout his career. He currently lives in Cedaredge, CO with his wife.

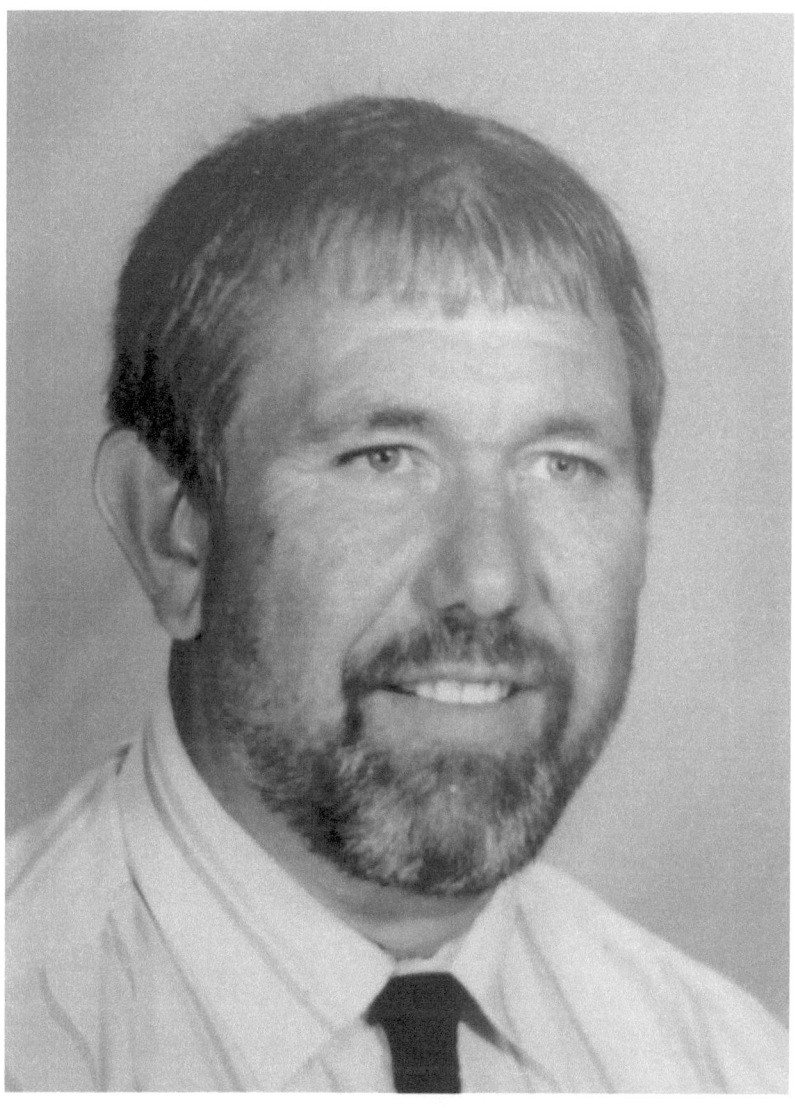

Also Available from Kellogg Press

Vacant Childhood
Lindsey Bartlett

He Watched and Took Note
Curtis Becker

Six Feet Apart: Poetry from the Pandemic
AJ Dome

Everything is Ephemera
Dennis Etzel, Jr.

Dirt Road
Kerry Moyer

Rust & Weeds
Kerry Moyer

I Love the Child
Ronda Miller

Winds of Time
Ronda Miller

Watch Your Head
Kevin Rabas

Watch Your Head 2
Kevin Rabas

Order online at kelloggpress.com

www.ingramcontent.com/pod-product-compliance
Lightning Source LLC
Chambersburg PA
CBHW031255290426
44109CB00012B/598